Duvet Days

PETER D HEHIR

THE CHOIR PRESS

First published in the United Kingdom in 2020 by
The Choir Press

ISBN 978-1-78963-156-2

'The Pen has been lifted,
The Ink has now dried,
So open your hearts
And see what's inside'

Peter D Hehir
2020

Contents

The World is Closed

(The Poem for the COVID-19 Pandemic 2020)

They said the world was closed today
So I went to have a look,
I found it with the shutters down
And the phone was off the hook.

So I stood there for a little while
But no one was around,
Then Silence came and startled me
With the most alarming sound.

I asked him where the others were,
And why the streets were bare,
He whispered 'Life had ran away
While Death was playing there.'

'Oh no' I said 'It can't be true
For Life is not afraid'
'But no one ever goes' he said
'Where Death has ever played.'

I understood and walked away
As Hope was standing there,
With Courage in her afterglow
And the sunlight in her hair.

She said 'Go home to those you love
This is no place to be,
For if we walk these streets today
Then no one shall be free'.

She threw her light to lead the way
And showed me where to go,
The very road that life had gone
Where the future flowers grow.

Then Death showed me another way
But I didn't want to look,
So I stumbled home in time for tea
And I read another book.

It was called *The World is Closed Today*
And the streets we shouldn't roam,
The first line said 'Just please be safe'
And the ending – 'Stay at Home.'

Evermore

To fairest Juliet I write
As stars lay back against the night
And all the world will come to see
How captivating beauty be.
And through her eyes that actors play,
To kiss the lips of yesterday,
Where once she gave her hand to mine
Like lovers lost in lovers time.
But as I reach with empty heart
Our aching hands are torn apart
And life will end but for a while,
As tears fall to drown a smile.
Yet I shall seek you 'til they dry
And tear the clouds out of the sky,
To show the world like once before
My want for you grows evermore.
But full my heart with false desire
That embers play in passions fire
And die like love with mystery;
How captivating beauty be?

Boxing Day in Birmingham

As I head on past the Bullring
With Christmas in my eyes,
Where the world awaits with plastic plates
Of yesterday's mince pies.

Then Noddy Holder sings again
As the crowds do not relent,
The voices say how much to pay?
So how much have I spent??

But walk I must and walk I do
With steps as small as time,
The trains are late but still they wait
With their complimentary wine.

So down towards Grand Central now
There's a choir by the doors,
There's queues for loos and sweets and booze
And there's sales in the stores.

Now the Pogues are on the stereos
With a fairytale or too,
There's prams all crammed on Christmas trams
With ankles black and blue.

There's bags all stuffed with emptiness
And ten pence at your leisure,
But all the doubt comes falling out
That we're doing this for pleasure.

For everything is half the price,
But we're all twice the size,
As I box my way through Boxing Day
With Christmas in my eyes.

Let's go a Marching

I write from the trenches
With a pen full of fear
And a shiver of sadness
Like the frost to the deer.

For the winter is harsh now,
Through the flame and the fire
And the only hands working
Are the clocks on the spire.

And the snow is a blanket
Where another dream goes,
But I can feel my heartbeat
In the tips of my toes.

So let's go a marching,
Go a marching they said,
Through the dirt and the debris
Past the dying and the dead.

Where the feelings are rationed
Less than three to a man,
When the night said we couldn't
But the day said we can.

Now I sit on these benches
With a prayer and a tear,
As the poppies wear raincoats
When there's nobody here.

Wonder

The curtain fell like Autumn
With crimson lace and bows,
As all the golden leaves performed
In moonlit tickled shows.

They asked but for an audience,
We had but not a thought,
To season, splash or songbird
And the wonders that they taught.

The blades of grass would sparkle,
Then die beneath our feet,
We'd stand there with our smiles on
In nature's great defeat.

But there's nothing left to look at
Now we've untied all the bows
And the curtain hides the winter
Where by every dreamer goes.

When the Sky gets Dark

Happy young lovers
Walk through the park,
Hide beneath the covers
When the sky gets dark.

Early dawn dancers
Glide on the frost,
Like sunrise romancers
With paradise lost.

Late night shoppers
Stroll through the town,
Like wine bottle stoppers
When the taste goes down.

Silver Star pickers
Gaze at the sky,
Like autumn leaf kickers
Where dreams don't die.

Drunken eyes wander
Like spirited souls,
Smile at the thunder
Where the last cloud rolls.

As old age writers
Carve up the bark,
With an army of lighters
When the sky gets dark.

Walney Island

Hard blows the wind of Walney
On an island full of dreams,
And waters flow to a place we know
In a world of submarines.

As Biggar Bank is beckoning
With a history of its own
And a ferry built to conquer silt
Just to take the travellers home.

With all those shipwreck stories,
As the harbour plays its part,
Just by the ridge of Jubilee Bridge
Where the sunset stole my heart.

Past all the ghosts of Vickerstown,
Where the tide just ebbs and flows,
We stroll on home, though not alone
As the wind of Walney blows.

Dimpleforth McMuckwind

A pleasant old fellow was Dimple
But he led a tragic life,
He was arrested late in '63
For trying to clone his wife.

He got so far when the police burst in
And found him standing there,
With Six Mrs McMuckwinds
Who all had ginger hair.

He claimed that he would sell them on
As cleaners, slaves and cooks
And that he'd found out how to clone
From Irish recipe books.

The police did not believe a word,
They read him all his rights
And placed him in a prison cell
For two whole days and nights.

Then when they came to check on him
He was as happy as could be,
For in the night he'd cloned himself
And set his double free.

But the real Dimple went to court
And was sentenced to serve life,
With himself, his wife, his wife
His wife, his wife, his wife, his wife.

Cynefin

Where a rusty old bicycle
Clings to the wall,
By a phone box of plant pots
That will fade in the fall.

As a blade of grass beckons
To a butterflies wings,
In the gardens all glowing
With such colourful things.

Where the wood peeled windows
Breathe through the moss,
As the wild wind whispers
By the old wooden cross.

Like an opened umbrella
When there's no rain at all,
Where a rusty old bicycle
Just clings to the wall.

You are ...

You are the salt to my chips
And the stars in my sky,
You are the kiss on my lips
And the X to my Y.

You are the ring to my finger
And the bird to my nest,
You are the song to my singer
And the heart in my chest.

You are the whit to my laughter
And the air to my balloon,
You are the film to my bafta
And the curve to my moon.

You are the pen to my paper
And the highs to my trips,
You are the light to my taper
And the salt on my chips.

The Town that Roofed the World

(An ode to Blaenau Ffestiniog)

Onwards down the hillside
Through valleys as we roll,
The air is filled with yesterdays
And the sweetest smell of coal.

Where treetops wave in wonder
And the embers fill the grate,
Where once the tracks were rumbling
With those wagons full of slate.

So onwards to Porthmadog,
Where the locomotives roam,
Beneath the steam filled canopy
We will soon be touching home.

To be sitting by the chimney Breast
Where the fireplace is filled,
With coal that came a chugging
From the Town that roofed the world.

Cancel the Flowers

Cancel the flowers
For my heart still beats,
Take in the bunting
And clear the streets.

Put down your glasses
And burst all the clouds,
Blow out the candles
And quieten the crowds.

Turn off the sunset,
Turn on the words,
And plug in the sunrise
With a song for the birds

Then pull up your anchors
Be bold and be free,
Cancel the flowers,
Think only of me.

The Lonely Lighthouse Keeper

On an island manned by a thousand dreams
Where a sunbeam lives and a raindrop gleams
And all is calm in the world it seems,
Where the daytime hides the stars.

And waves just crash on the crying rocks,
Where neither a saint nor a fisherman docks,
There's a hole in his soul that matches his socks,
Like he tiptoes on cigars.

Where the light shines on like a man made moon,
As the wind whistles past like a flying platoon
And the flowers below are dying too soon,
Like a life inside a vase.

In this lighthouse built on a thousand beams,
Like the captains of opposing teams,
Where all is calm in the world it seems
But the night time hides the scars.

Elastic

There's a dent in your confidence
A blocker in your flow,
You're living on the breadline
As the world is passing go.

Now you can't get out of jail
'Til you roll another double,
You said you didn't planet
But it got you into Hubble.

Your world is full of enemies
And friends you never knew,
Your sole has got a hole in
And the waters coming through.

You're wrist is full of watches
But we know they're second hand,
You call yourself elastic
Like the singer of a band.

Now there's flowers in your garden
But the borders under guard,
Your trees are slowly folding
Into paper and to card.

So you take up origami
But the paper cuts attack
And your phone has got a tap on
With a message on the back.

So you buy a newer model
But the signals still the same,
You roll a pair of snakes' eyes
And you're back into the game.

Then the wolves begin to gather
Like demons at your door,
So you hide behind the story
And you move to number four.

Because the Fairytale tells you
That's where you won't be found,
As you watch two other houses
Go tumbling to the ground.

So you give away your watches
Just to kill a bit of time
And you swap them for a diamond
Like a sentence for a crime.

Now those carrots on your fingers
Could melt a snowman's heart,
You tried to walk on water
But the waves would never part.

So you turned into a joker,
Like the leader of the pack
And you shuffle through this city
Like a Rose without a Jack.

But the struggles still Titanic
And your ship is going down,
In a bottle full of whiskey
Where the dreamers never drown.

Tuesday

It rained on Tuesday afternoon
Just like they said it would,
As all we saw there by the moon
Were footsteps in the mud.

The stars appeared brighter still
As daylight closed its eyes,
With shadows on the window sill
Where wonder never dies.

As puddles splashed the garden fence
And the snails took a bath,
By the ballad of a fifty pence
That lay upon the path.

And the guilty went where sinners sinned
Like snowflakes in the flood,
As autumn whispered to the wind
Just like they said it would.

Cecil

(In Memory of Cecil the Lion)

Where once you roamed a gentle soul,
With a fierce face and eyes of coal,
But ever still the beast you were
Like a loving king in a lions fur.

You gave a smile to a world in awe
And shouted back with a gentle roar,
Then raised your cubs on the barrow land
Where humans sit and lions stand.

But now you've gone just time remains
And human hands show bloody stains,
So goodnight Cecil and rest in peace,
You remain a king in a golden fleece.

V.A.R

(Virus Altering Reality –
As Sport was cancelled during The Pandemic of 2020)

We'll have to take a little break
As we check with V.A.R,
We're the players socially distancing
As it went in off the bar?

They're looking at the monitors
The crowd is rather tense,
For we can't see the very thing
That's breaching our defence.

The replays come around again,
Like three weeks at a time,
For we must stand and wait a while
The right side of the line.

The whistle blows, decision made,
We disconnect the Zoom,
The V.A.R check is complete
And play can now resume.

The Ghost of Cannock Chase

Play hide and seek with me my love
In the trees of Cannock Chase,
Where the barks are carved with memories
That no one can replace.

The air here smells of older times
In the splinters of the light,
Where moonbeams shine forever on
The playground of the night.

We're not alone within these woods
With frost upon the nettle,
There are feet that walk the forest floor
Where the footprints try to settle.

So do not hide too long my love
In the trees of Cannock Chase,
For the blackest eyes are watching you
From a playful child's face.

The Phoenix

When the sun sets on your shoulders
And you're cursed with tired eyes,
Just take a stroll where the pennies roll
And the laughter never dies.

When the starlight sees you crying
In your evening suit disguise,
Just glance away to yesterday
Where a sleeping memory lies.

When the shadows see you running
As the moonlight slowly dies,
Let silhouettes do pirouettes
In the longest of goodbyes.

When the sunrise sees you smiling
Like it caught you by surprise,
Just stand and stare without a care
Where the phoenix never flies.

Complete

Your kisses ran wild
Like the ivy that climbs,
Up the walls of my heart
Through the happiest times.

As your love whispered to me
Then you shouted aloud,
When you drew on my skyline
Such a beautiful cloud.

Which came with a rainbow
That tickled my soul,
You completed my puzzle
Just by making me whole.

For you are such a beauty
Made of nature's design,
Now I give you my walls
For your ivy to climb.

Re: Cycled

I marked another photo
With a comment and a like,
I cycled through the pictures
Like a camera on a bike.
I tagged you in a status
And gave you all the hype,
But the font that I was using
It just never was my type.
So I removed all of the comments
And took them from your wall,
Like scrubbing off graffiti –
There was nothing left at all.
So I uploaded a smile
And you downloaded a frown,
We added friends of friends who knew
A friend from out of town.
Then all we saw were memories
That the night before forgot,
With albums full of characters
Who would never know the plot.
So I simply cycled backwards
Like a camera on a bike,
Just collecting all the negatives
With a comment and a like.

Juliet

Dear Juliet we did not die
Nor should they mourn the place you lie,
For 'twas not them nor you nor eye
That taught the morning bird to cry.

And as thy candle rages light,
So soft against the darkest night,
To burn and burn a raging white
That feathered quill shall fall in flight.

But be not still that heart of mine
For blood shall flow where mourners dine,
Like vessels made to carry wine,
To time untouched of untouched time.

Dear Romeo you did not die
Nor should they mourn the place you lie,
For "twas thy lovers passing by
That taught the morning bird to fly.

Fly

Spread your wings like buttercups
To welcome in the rain,
And let those eyes that stare at you
See beauty in your pain.

Go show the world your coloured soul
And kiss me as you leave,
Let every season sun that sets
Be a pillow when you grieve.

Then carry whispers on with you
To the darkest points you know
And don't forget to think of me
In the sunbeams or the snow.

So fly my love to the highest peaks
Where no one knows your name,
Go spread your wings like buttercups
To welcome in the rain.

Monochrome Magic

A purple sound comes humming
In a yellow dawns full bloom,
As red eyes read the rising
Of another marbled moon.
And the jagged, blinding whiteness
That crowned the sightless night
Sleeps above blue heaven
In the rainbows prism light.
As green life lifts and stretches,
Aqua waves anoint the shore,
Brown bodies kneel and kiss the earth,
Black yields to blue once more.

We are Mosaics

We are mosaics
Piece by piece,
We are the wrinkles
Crease by crease.
We are the footsteps
Tread by tread,
We are the fabric
Thread by thread.
We are the soldiers
War by war,
We are the rivers
Thaw by thaw.
We are the cannons
Shot by shot,
We are survivors
Knot by knot.
We are the stories
Page by page,
We are the actors
Stage by stage.
We are the silence
Shout by shout,
We are the water
Drought by drought.
We are the pilgrims
Race by race,
We are the mountains
Face by face.
We are the seasons
Light by light,

We are the courage
Fight by fight.
We are the chapters
Part by part,
We are the lovers
Heart by heart.
We are the poems
Line by line,
We are the Chalice
And we are the Wine.

Upon Bluebell Wood

I called for you but no one came,
So in the oak I carved your name,
And every day I did the same,
I called for you but no one came.

I searched for you but couldn't see,
So I carved again into the tree
A heart so you remember me,
I searched for you couldn't see.

I longed for you but waited still
And gave my name that space to fill,
Upon that tree beside the hill,
I longed for you but waited still.

I called once more but no one came,
So from the oak I took your name,
And watched it burn into the flame,
I called for you but no one came.

The Last Days of Romance

As the vultures kissed the cannibals
And our eyes began to dance,
At the feast of the long lost animals
In the last days of romance.

So despair the lies of winters,
In the snowy hills we climb
And our soul is full of splinters
That will torture us in time.

But be not sad when war salutes
In the mourning of desire,
When legends fall like parachutes
In the burning of the fire.

When the soldiers ripped the pages
From the books we never read,
So Rejoice! The vulture rages,
Now the cannibals are dead.

EU In or EU Out?

You can keep your Spanish bull fights
And your Danish bacon too,
For we don't need these politics
To tell us what to do.

You can have back all your Brussels sprouts
And keep your German cars,
We can live without the Irish craic
And those noisy Spanish bars.

You can keep Republics all in Czech,
And your 'au revoir et oui',
From Latvia to Luxembourg
It's all just Greek to me.

You can keep Croatian scenery,
And the stunning Maltese crest,
You can claim back ABBA as your own,
From Rome to Budapest.

You can keep the slopes of Austria
For we find it rather cold,
We will give back every Windmill house
That the Netherlands has sold.

You can have your Tallinn old town,
And your Bratislavan days,
You can keep the Northern Lights that play
In the dying Finnish haze.

You can have back your Romania,
And the colourful Bucharest,
Then when you're feeling Hungary-
Did I mention Budapest?

You can have back Ljubljana
And it's lack of many vowels,
You can search for answers once again
Like a Parliament of owls.

But from Warsaw, Walsall or Westminster
The choice is up to you,
For we don't need these politics
To tell us what to do.

Everest

As the sun pulls back the covers
On this graveyard in the sky,
Where the few went to the summit
But the many came to die.

Like souls beneath an avalanche
As time released the rope,
From hands that froze in emptiness
But thawed again in hope.

And nature bows in empathy
At the echoes gone before,
As the clouds release a memory
From a sky that fought the war.

Now the snowflakes gather knowingly
Where the brave and buried lie,
As the moon puts back the covers
On this graveyard in the sky.

Red Light River

Broken Windscreen Wipers
Will wave us out of town,
As engines hiss like vipers
When I turn the music down.

And the wheels roll like cigarettes
On the tarmac full of rain,
With potholes full of no regrets
That catch us out again.

As thoughts just turn to coffee cups
Where warmth begins to play
And cupboards full of pick me ups
To keep the sleep away.

But the darkness plays a shiver
On the top lip of a frown,
Across this red light river,
As the rain keeps coming down.

Murder by Moonlight

And It started with the end,
But was crippled by design,
A body wrapped in emptiness
By a broken glass of wine.

When shadows stood in silence
As the embers laced the fire,
By the crumpled claret carpet
With a life of lost desire.

But No one saw the passing
Where the sinner came to play,
In a scene devoid of loneliness
For the killer not the prey.

And It ended with the start,
When the neighbourhood awakes,
He left the scene so cunningly
As the cat flap gently shakes.

By the Dying of the Light

Where the street lamps tease a shadows soul
And the swallows take to flight,
With lips to temper and console
By the dying of the light.

Where the leaves curl up to die again,
In a bittersweet defeat,
By benches sat in splintered pain
Where hearts began to beat.

As the blackbird sings a lonely tune
To rage against the night,
Where love was taken far too soon
By the dying of the light.

April

Where a flower blooms
As the daylight breathes,
And the winter sun
Rolls down its sleeves.

Where the Ivy climbs
Up a garden wall,
And the children play
Where the shadows fall.

Where the branches curve
Like a newborn smile,
As daffodils stretch
To the sky for a while.

Where the splinters break
Through a thousand leaves,
As the springtime sun
Rolls up its sleeves.

Apples and Androids

My heart feels like December
Now it's snowing in my bones,
There's passers by with either eye
On nothing but their phones.

The snow is falling quicker now
But it barely hits the ground,
As those fingers write a tweet tonight
Where their followers are found.

With Christmas candles flickering
As a moth plays with the flame,
There's party hosts and Facebook posts
That all just sound the same.

And the stars will stay awake tonight
On this drowning world of tones,
Where your feelings swam to Instagram
As it's snowing in your bones.

When the Lights were Low

Where did you go when the lights were low?
Through the amber leaves and the afterglow,
As you fell asleep beneath the snow,
Where did you go when the lights were low?

Where did you stay at the close of day?
In the final scene of a fateful play,
You left the stage as the pages say,
Where did you stay at the close of day?

Where did you hide when the sunset died?
Through the burning sky and the pain inside,
When the day gave in and the stars replied,
Where did you hide when the sunset died?

So where did you go when the lights were low?
Through the amber leaves and the afterglow,
Just rest your head beneath the snow
And I will see you soon when the lights are low.

Watercolours

Put the clouds in blankets
Turn off the setting sun,
And sit with me at nightfall
Where the watercolours run.

Count the very raindrops
That soak the very skin,
And rage against the dying light
A war we couldn't win.

Then breathe into the wild
And Look up at the stars,
Like lovers watching silhouettes
From the bonnets of there cars.

Then give the day it's encore
And when the night is done,
Just sit with me at sunrise
Like we've only just begun.

Chapter, Verse and Curtain Calls

Where a bookworm lives on a written page,
Where words break out from a paper cage,
As Ink is stretched on the biggest stage,
In a Library full of dreams.

Where spines will tingle in your palm
Like a storm of prose on a sea of calm,
As rustic smells unleash their charm
With magic at the seams.

Then fiction bursts where eyes react
With stories bound by fun and fact,
In covers kissed and paper backed
Where the punctuation gleams.

Then bookmarks rest where silence falls
Through Chapter, Verse and Curtain Calls,
There are stories etched within these walls,
In a Library full of dreams.

Cancer

You give us all such heartache
Now the world is feeling down,
You creep inside and try to hide
In this circus like a clown.

But we find you in the corner
With another room to fill
And then you rage inside the cage
Like a hunter at the kill.

Then we try our best to beat you
When you silently appear,
And we guard the door just like before
As you're not allowed in here.

So don't look back when leaving,
You're not welcome anymore,
As you might be winning battles
But you'll never win the war.

Marmite

Love me or hate me it has to be said
I taste good on crackers or wholemeal bread.
I divide all opinion because of my taste,
Use me with pleasure; discard me with haste.
But I might be the last thing when cupboards are bare
So use me, abuse me and spread me with care.
Then love me or hate me it has to be said;
I taste good on crackers or wholemeal bread.

I Am Love

I am the thunder that sets the sparrowhawks to flight,
I am the flame that flickers soft against the night,
I am the wind beneath the wings of every kite,
I am Love, I am Love.

I am diamonds sitting proud on every ring,
I am music when the world forgets to sing,
I am whispers when you didn't say a thing,
I am Love, I am Love.

I am the smiles and the tears in your eyes,
I am freedom in another new disguise,
I am trying on your laughter lines for size,
I am Love, I am Love.

I am flowers in a garden full of weeds,
I am colour where you never scattered seeds,
I am everything a person ever needs,
I am Love, I am Love.

Climbing over Sunsets

Like a world within a raindrop
Or a sky without a star,
I am climbing over sunsets
Just to get to where you are.

Like a cellar with the lights on
Or a train track in the dark,
I am waiting like that sycamore
In the corner of the park.

Like a spine without a shiver,
Or a burning wooden heart
I will drift on like a satellite
Until I find the missing part.

Like a world within a raindrop
Or a wish that travelled far,
I am risking every sunrise
Just to get to where you are.

The Deep Unkind

When the whistle blows leave your heart behind
Write your message in the dust,
When the enemy shows and the world goes blind
Let your helmets turn to rust.

When the stars relent and the splinter breaks
Like the falling light of dawn,
When your back is bent and your body aches
And your soul is lost and torn.

When the shelling stops and the frost appears
Where the flowers grew before,
When a smile drops under heavy tears
Where the flowers grow no more.

Where the ill wind blows in the deep unkind
And all life has lost its trust,
When that whistle blows leave your heart behind
And the helmets turn to rust.

When The Floods Came

In the mildest ever winter
When the roads turned into rivers,
And the people clung to lamp-posts,
As their hugs turned into shivers.

As the cars became the sugar cubes
In a swirling pot of tea,
As we opened up the curtains
And we gazed on out to sea.

Yet not a soul is swimming
And the water hides the smiles,
There's emotions on the rip tide
And they're stretching out for miles.

But our hearts have great defences,
As we drink from broken mugs,
You can be somebody's lamp-post,
Turning shivers into hugs.

Stardust

When she smiles nothing matters
But that look upon her face,
As the stardust slowly shatters
Where the beauty couldn't trace.

Then she laughs like angels playing
With an orchestra in tune,
To the sound of starlight saying
That they long to see the moon.

And her heart is full of kisses
For there's loving under there,
By a thousand perfect wishes
That her soul just wants to share.

Then she smiles; nothing matters,
For the worlds a better place,
Where the stardust slowly shatters
In the beauty on her face.

Snowflakes

The high street's closed to traffic
So we're drifting down the road,
Like a pair of winter snowflakes
That have no fixed abode.

There are lights in all the windows
Like the ones we've never seen,
As Jack Frost paints graffiti
On the places we have been.

Then we fall into temptation
As the chestnuts slowly roast
And the crowds begin to shiver
Like they're hugging Marley's ghost.

As the frost nips at our noses
And the world will say it snowed,
Now the high street's closed to traffic
As were drifting down the road.

Dancing with the Devil

I was dancing with Devil
When an angel stopped the band
And the spirits took the level
So much higher than we planned.

Then the waltzers moved like fire
As the sound of love returned,
On a dancefloor of desire
Where the candle never burned.

And the night returned the singers
To the limelight once again,
As pianos wait for fingers
By a river of champagne.

Then the curtains started closing
As the crowds began to leave,
I was dancing with the Devil
With a joker up my sleeve.

Paper Cuts

Set your ship to sail upon my seas,
Use my hands to pull you from your knees
And I will be the cure to your disease,
Now set your ship to sail upon my seas.

Then use my coat to shelter from the rain,
And let me kiss those paper cuts again,
When all those pages crumple up in pain,
Use my coat to shelter from the rain.

And let your lion dance into my lair,
I'll run my tired fingers through your hair
And when you're lost just know that I'll be there,
So let your lion dance into my lair.

Then let your lips run wild upon my skin,
I will celebrate the day when lovers win,
So close the door and let no others in,
Then let your lips run wild upon my skin.

Grass Stains

Lay on the leaves with me
By the ballet of dragonflies,
Walk on your knees with me
Where the weeping willow lies.

Stare at the clouds with me
Where the storytellers create,
Crawl through the crowds with me
Like the bird that is too late.

Come pick out the flowers with me
On a carpet full of dreams,
And sit here for hours with me
With flakes in our ice creams.

Then curl up and sneeze with me
As the pollen hurts our eyes,
Just lay on those leaves with me
By the ballet of dragonflies.

They Don't Knock Twice

There's a building in the backstreet
With your name above the door,
There's a ghost outside the entrance
And he's been there once before.

With chains around his ankles
And desire in his eyes,
His soul is made of memories
Where the demon never dies.

He gazes through the spy-hole
To watch you as you walk,
In a doorway full of whispers
Where the lonely never talk.

But this one still remembers
Now he's knocking at your door,
So bolt them creaking locks again
Like you never have before.

Curzon Street

(In Honour of the Historic Birmingham Train Station)

There are ghosts all drunk on red, red wine
Just waiting on the city line,
To catch a train that never comes
Past tired eyes and pigeon crumbs.

The tracks all ache with metal screams
Of Journeys to a million dreams,
But they return with nightmares still
If actions spoke and looks could kill

Then antique hearts would be at rest
Inside a tired travellers chest,
Where pulses raced upon the rails
To hopes of heads but throwing tails.

And now these ghosts no longer wait
For trains in Eighteen Thirty-Eight,
Instead they drag their angry feet
Past the waiting queues of Curzon Street.

Hunting for Kisses

I went hunting for kisses
Then your smile ran wild,
And the beauty just sparkled
Like the eyes of a child.

As my fingers drew love lines
To the curves of your soul,
And my heart made a tremor
As your kiss made me whole.

Then I ventured on further
Through the doubt of a touch,
But I whispered 'I'm here
And I miss you as much.'

So just swim in my sunset,
I have made it so mild,
I went hunting for kisses
Then your smile ran wild.

The Undertones of Magic

Like the undertones of magic
Running through my veins,
Washing off the history
And all its tragic stains.

Like instruments for melodies
We're played until we play,
That broken watch you never fixed
Is right but twice a day.

Like leaves upon the autumn wind
We have no place to fall,
And never a place to grow again
When winter comes to call.

Like the undertones of magic
That forever promised peace,
To all us tenants of the earth
Who can't renew the lease.

The Fairytale Begins

(A Very Brummy Christmas)

It's Christmas Eve in Birmingham
And there's panic on the streets,
There's old charades and Christmas cards
And a box of chocolate treats.

There are wise men holding shopping bags
Such hope is in their eyes,
It's getting late but still they wait
Forlorn and not so wise.

Then hours pass like people do
And the city fills with souls,
Just rushing by beneath the sky
Where another winter rolls.

But your fingers smell of sellotape
And the markets smell of wine
That warms your hands by burger stands
As the hungry wait in line.

So you make your way back home again
Where the fireplace is lit
And you start to rest by the chimney breast
Where Santa couldn't fit.

Then up those steps to happy dreams
And the Fairytale begins,
Where the morning fights the Christmas lights
But the night time never wins.

Now it's Christmas Day in Birmingham
And the wrapping papers torn,
So we sit on seats to watch repeats
Until another year is born.

Trouble Never Travels Alone

Trouble never travels alone
For it rides a horse and cart,
It will twist its knife like winters wife
And tear your world apart.

Trouble never travels alone
As it rides its way through town,
It will fill your pockets with diamonds and lockets
And turn you upside down.

Trouble never travels alone
As it tiptoes over streams,
It will creep right in where the walls are thin
To kidnap all your dreams.

Trouble never travels alone
For it rides a horse and cart,
It will beg and borrow with two for sorrow
As it wears the devils heart.

Bleeding Heart

At the haunting of my bleeding heart
There was nothing left but love,
And time resets as souls depart
Where the skyline meets the dove.

Now the basements creak of yesterday's
When tomorrow never comes,
As pulses raced in red displays
To the beating of the drums.

And sunshine left this tired soul
To a heartbeat of its own,
With all the footsteps that it stole
Being left to walk alone.

Then the jigsaw mourned its missing part
Like a hand that left the glove,
At the haunting of my bleeding heart
There was nothing left but love.

Papillon

So weeds must grow
On drunken soil,
But still you flow
A scene to spoil,
And not by you
But birds that pass,
Where once you flew
And went alas;
Like fall of day
To dark descent,
In bold display
Of blue repent.
Yet once you go
Where lights recoil,
So weeds must grow
On drunken soil.

When the War is Over

Your rocking chair is empty now
But your book's still on the side,
Of how to kill a mockingbird
And the many times you've tried.

There are battles by the fireplace
That only you can quell,
And stories in the tallest trees
That only you can tell.

There are whispers in the basement
That only you can hear,
With your smile like a canopy
To catch a dying tear.

But when the war is over
And the rocking chairs are still,
I will write another memory
For the mockingbird to kill.

Will we grow old Together?

Will we grow old together,
Through the wrinkles and the pain?
When our grey hair shows
Like the winter snows,
On the cars of memory lane.

Will we grow old together,
Like the pictures that we drew?
Of the old oak trees
In the summer breeze,
Knowing things we never knew.

Will we grow old together,
As the seasons all retire?
To spend our days
Where the reaper plays,
Like blackbirds on the wire.

Will we grow old together,
Through the raindrops and the sun?
Where the light will shine
On the vintage wine,
That we will both become.